# Contents

Contents

## Special Features

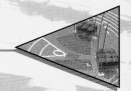

## Features

Safari **POWER**

**Poetry Corner**

**Safari Cooking**

**Safari Travel**

**readingsafari.com**

# The History of the Olympics

Written by Kerrie Capobianco

The Olympics are an international sports festival. The first Olympics were held in ancient Greece. The earliest recorded date of the Olympics is 776 BC, although many historians believe they began many centuries before that time.

Athens, Greece

# The Ancient Olympics

Athletics played a very important role in the religious festivals of the ancient Greeks. Historians think that athletic competitions were held for the funerals of important people. Later, the competitions became part of religious festivals.

An Olympic athlete enters the temple of Zeus at Olympia.

The Greek games were held every four years in the stadium at Olympia. These Olympics were for male athletes and male spectators.

For many years, the only event that was in the ancient Olympics was a footrace of about 210 yards (192 m). This was the length of the stadium.

From 708 to 648 BC, other sports were added to the games. These sports included the pentathlon, with jumping, running, discus and javelin throws, and wrestling.

Ancient Greece was conquered by the Romans during the 140s BC. In AD 393, the Roman Emperor Theodosius I ended the Olympics. It would be more than 1,500 years before the games would start again.

# The Modern Olympics

A Frenchman named Baron Pierre de Coubertin believed that the Olympics would help promote international goodwill. In 1894, Pierre de Coubertin presented his ideas to an international sports convention in Paris. The group liked his ideas, and formed the International Olympic Committee.

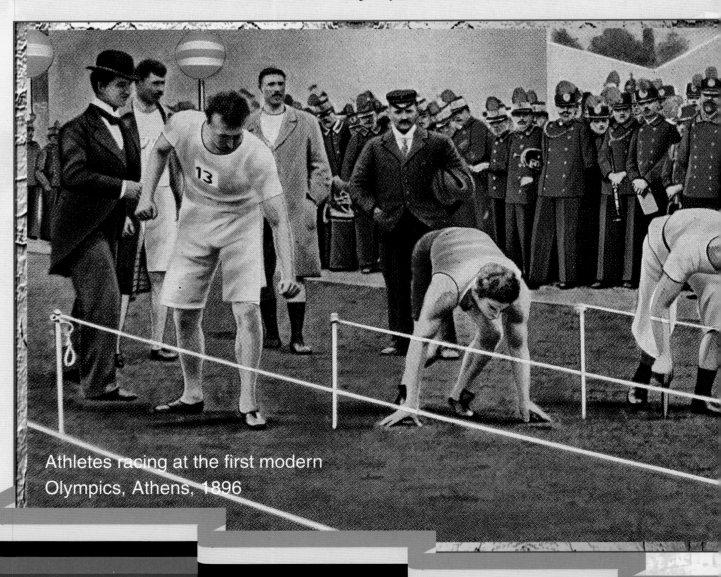

Athletes racing at the first modern Olympics, Athens, 1896

The first modern Olympics took place in Athens, Greece, in 1896. There were nine sports: cycling, fencing, gymnastics, lawn tennis, shooting, swimming, track and field, weightlifting, and wrestling.

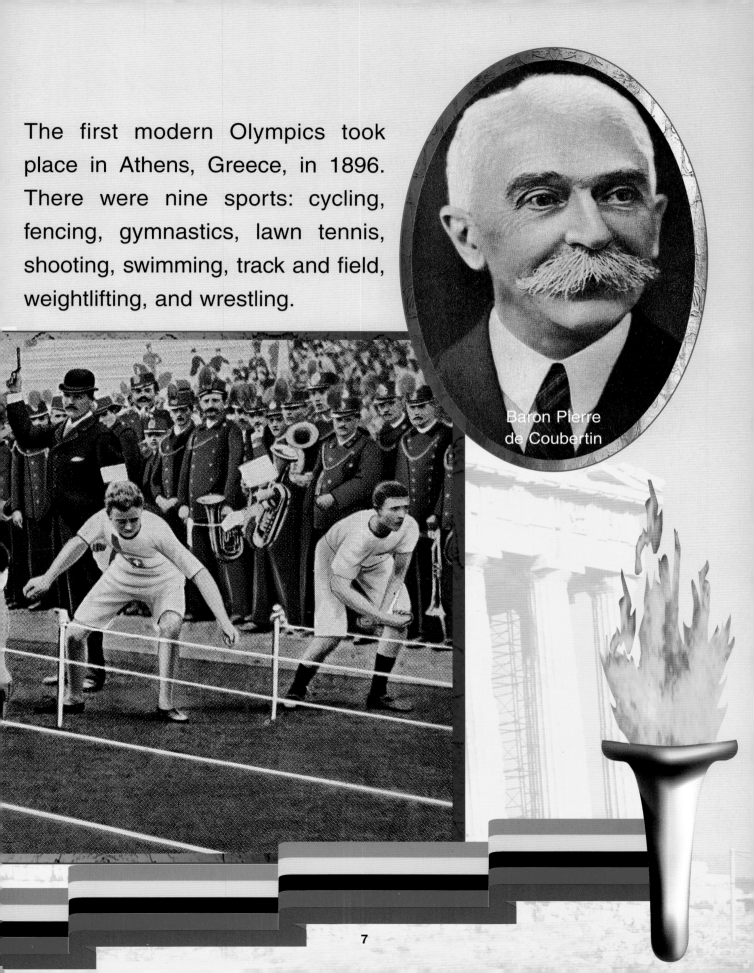

Baron Pierre de Coubertin

# The Winter Olympics

In 1924, the Winter Olympics began. At first, they were held during the same year as the Summer Olympics. In 1994 this was changed. Now, the Winter Olympics are held every four years, two years after the Summer Olympics.

Snowboarding

Ice hockey is one of the events at the Winter Olympics.

Skiing

Some events that are included in the Winter Olympics are alpine and Nordic skiing, ski jumping, luge, ice hockey, figure skating, speed skating, bobsledding, snowboarding, curling, and biathlon, with shooting and cross-country skiing.

Speed skaters at the Winter Olympics

# Safari POWER

**Word Meanings**

*a, b, or c?*

anthem
- **a** – *ant trail*
- **b** – *song*
- **c** – *necklace*

equestrian
- **a** – *throwing a metal ball*
- **b** – *horse riding*
- **c** – *running a long way*

festival
- **a** – *car*
- **b** – *film*
- **c** – *celebration*

oath
- **a** – *grain*
- **b** – *promise*
- **c** – *cheese*

participate
- **a** – *take part*
- **b** – *run away*
- **c** – *swing*

spectator
- **a** – *glasses*
- **b** – *magazine*
- **c** – *onlooker*

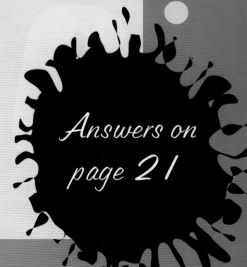

*Answers on page 21*

# The Gymnast

Written by Josephine Selwyn

The gymnast hangs
And swings
From the rings.

The gymnast walks
And leaps
On the beam.

The gymnast twists
And twirls
On the bars.

The gymnast jumps
And flips
On the horse.

The gymnast tumbles
And tumbles
And tumbles
And tumbles on the floor.

# At the
# Opening Ceremony

Written by Athena Tabakas

Illustrated by Bryan Pollard

I am so excited! I am here with my family at the opening ceremony of the Olympics!

There are so many people here! We are sitting in our seats waiting for the parade to begin. It will be a long time before we can move again because we have to wait and see all the athletes from the competing countries parade into the stadium.

My parents really wanted to bring us to see this ceremony. They said we might not get another chance, so they have saved and saved for four years so that we can be here.

It's such a special day for us because we used to live in the country that will come into the stadium first. That country is Greece. Greece always comes in first because the Olympics were first held many years ago in ancient Greece.

The country where the games are being held is called the host country. This year the country that is our new home is the host country. I am so proud because I can now cheer for two countries!

"How do the other countries know when to come into the stadium?" I asked my mother.

"They come into the stadium in alphabetical order," my mother replied. "The countries with names beginning with the letter A, like Argentina and Austria, come in first. The last ones are the countries with names beginning with the letter Z, like Zambia and Zimbabwe."

AUSTRALIA

"When all the athletes are in the stadium the games will be declared open," said my father.

"Then the Olympic flag will be raised. The flag has five rings that are joined together. The rings are blue, yellow, black, green, and red. The rings stand for the continents of Africa, Asia, Australia, Europe, and the Americas," said my mother.

"I wonder who will bring in the Olympic torch," said my brother. "We were told at school that relay runners have been bringing the Olympic flame all the way from Olympia."

"We'll have to wait and see," said my mother. "What else did you learn about the opening ceremony?"

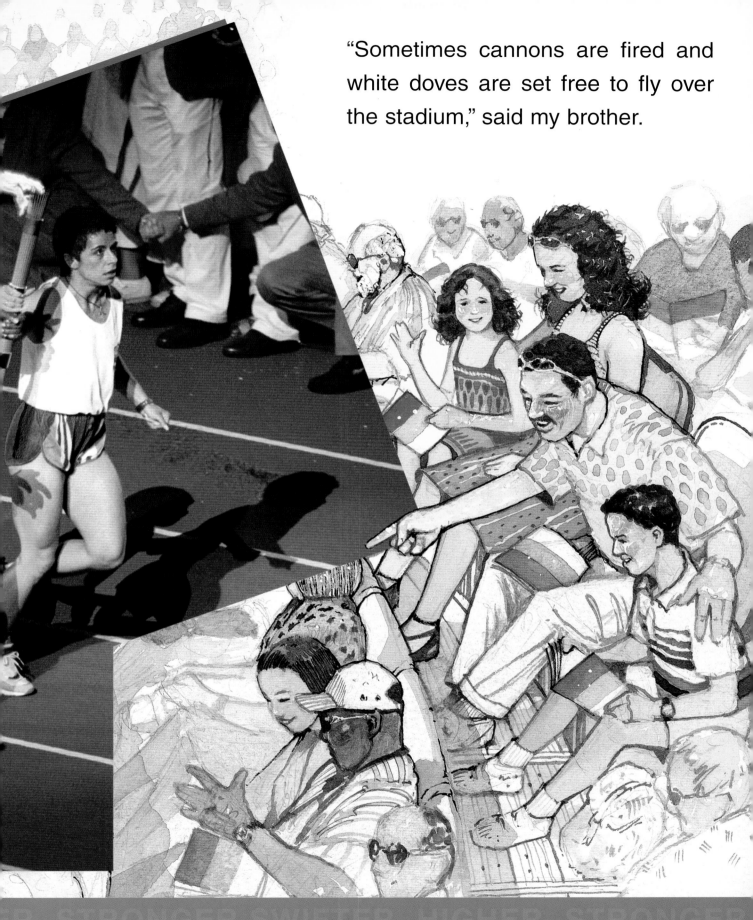

"Sometimes cannons are fired and white doves are set free to fly over the stadium," said my brother.

"The athletes will take the Olympic oath,"
I said. "They will promise to be good
sports and obey all the rules."

Just then, the ceremony started. We all stood up to sing our new national anthem. I felt so proud. I squeezed my mother's hand. "Thank you for bringing us," I said.

# Safari

## Cook

### Olympic Chickpea Dip

2 cups of cooked chickpeas

2/3 cup of tahini (sesame paste)

3/4 cup of lemon juice

2 cloves of garlic

Put all the ingredients in a food processor and mix to a smooth paste. Serve with crackers or raw vegetables.

# Safari

## Travel

### Olympic Tours

**Come to the Olympics with us.**

Our travel packages include flights, hotel rooms, and tickets to your choice of Olympic events.

Book now. Tickets selling fast.

···· For all your tour needs

# Safari POWER

**anthem**
**b** – song

**equestrian**
**b** – horse riding

**festival**
**c** – celebration

**oath**
**b** – promise

**participate**
**a** – take part

**spectator**
**c** – onlooker

*Xtra for Xperts*

*What is a pentathlon?*

## Rating Scale
5-6 Excellent    3-4 Very good    2 Good    0-1 Try again

# The *Decathlon*

Written by Sonny Reuben • Illustrated by Martin Bailey

**Day 1**

## Characters

**Event 1**   **Event 2**   **Event 3**   **Event 4**   **Event 5**

**Day 2**

**Event 6**   **Event 7**   **Event 8**   **Event 9**   **Event 10**

## Event 1

The decathlon is a sports event for men. It lasts for two days and has ten events. There are running, jumping, and throwing events in the decathlon. I am event number one. I am the 100-meter dash. The men have to sprint 100 meters. To sprint means that they have to run as fast as they can.

## Event 2

I am a jumping event. I am the long jump. The men have to jump as far as they can. They run fast along a runway and jump from a take-off board. They jump in the air and stretch out their legs. They land in a special sandpit.

### Event 3

I am a throwing event. I am called the shot put. The men hold a metal ball that they rest on one of their shoulders. The men crouch down, turn, and throw the shot put as far as they can.

### Event 4

I am another jumping event. I am the high jump. The men run up to the bar and jump as high as they can. They turn their bodies so that their heads and then their backs go over the bar before their feet. The men land on a well-padded mat.

### Event 5

I am another running race. This time the men have to run 400 meters. This means that they have to run once around the track. I am the last event on day one.

### Event 6

I am the first event on day two. I am a jumping event. I am a race to see who can run and jump over ten hurdles the fastest.

## Event 7

I am another throwing event. I am the discus. The men hold the discus against one of their hands and their arm. They turn, twist, and then throw the discus as far as they can.

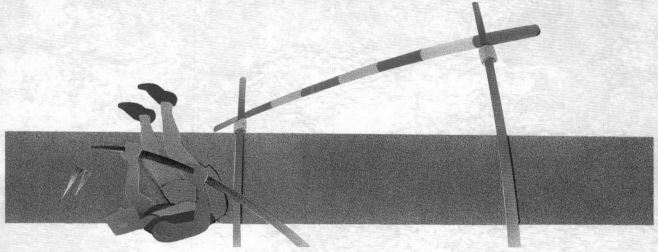

## Event 8

I am the pole vault. I am another jumping event. This time the men use a pole to help them jump very high off the ground over a bar. The men land on a well-padded mat.

## Event 9

I am another throwing event. I am the javelin throw. The men run down a track holding the javelin. At the throwing line they stretch back one of their arms and throw the javelin as far as they can.

## Event 10

I am the last race. I am the 1,500 meters. I am a running race. I am the longest running race in the decathlon. The athletes run around the track four times before they cross the finishing line.

## All the Events

We like being part of the decathlon. We meet lots of athletes. Some athletes are better at running and some athletes are better at jumping and some athletes are better at throwing.

At the end of the two days, the best athlete is the one who is good at all the events.

# Who Am I

Written by Simone Santo

I run
Fast as the wind,
Flat tack
On the track.
Who am I?

I throw.
I twirl and turn
And throw
As far as it will go.
Who am I?

I jump,
Run, hop, step, jump.
I land in sand,
Bump!
Who am I?

I swim,
Water in my eyes,
Arms
Like butterflies.
Who am I?

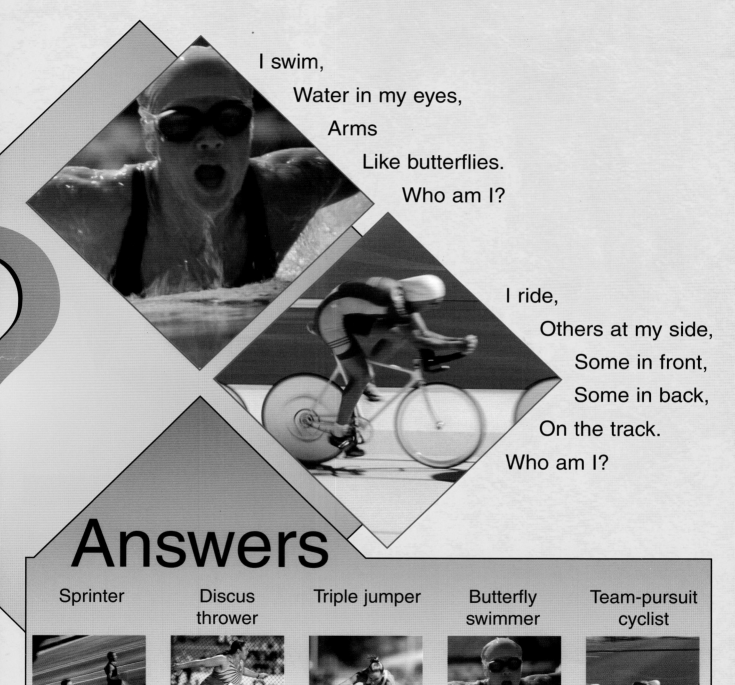

I ride,
Others at my side,
Some in front,
Some in back,
On the track.
Who am I?

# Answers

| Sprinter | Discus thrower | Triple jumper | Butterfly swimmer | Team-pursuit cyclist |

# readingsafari.com

## Check out these Safari magazines, too!

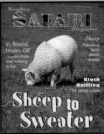

### Have your say -

e-mail your Safari Tour Guide at
tourguide@readingsafari.com

Safari Tour Guide, 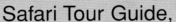 40

I like to watch equestrian events at the Olympics. I would like to ride at the Olympics one day.

Martina Harrison (8)

Find some fun things to do!

Go to –
http://www.readingsafari.com

## Safari *Superstar*

Name – Event 1

Birthday – March 17

Find out more about this Safari Superstar at
**http://www.readingsafari.com**